FIVE LITTLE DUCKS

Retold by STEVEN ANDERSON

Illustrated by KLAUS BIPPER

CANTATA
LEARNING

WWW.CANTATALEARNING.COM

CANTATA LEARNING

Published by Cantata Learning
1710 Roe Crest Drive
North Mankato, MN 56003
www.cantatalearning.com

Library of Congress Control Number: 2015932797
Anderson, Steven
    Five Little Ducks / retold by Steven Anderson; Illustrated by Klaus Bipper
    Series: Sing-along Math Songs
    Audience: Ages: 3–8; Grades: PreK–3
    Summary: Where are the five little ducks going? Count backward from five in
this classic song as the ducklings wander away from Mama Duck.
    ISBN: 978-1-63290-383-9 (library binding/CD)
    ISBN: 978-1-63290-514-7 (paperback/CD)
    ISBN: 978-1-63290-544-4 (paperback)
    1. Stories in rhyme. 2. Counting—fiction. 3. Ducks (Ducklings)—fiction.

Book design and art direction, Tim Palin Creative
Editorial direction, Flat Sole Studio
Music direction, Elizabeth Draper
Music arranged and produced by Steven C Music

Printed in the United States of America in North Mankato, Minnesota.
122015   0326CGS16

Ducklings usually stay close to their mother. But sometimes they **wander** off. Count backward from five as Mama Duck calls out for her ducklings to come home. **Quack**! Quack!

To find out if they return,
turn the page and sing along!

Five little ducks went out one day,
over the hills and far away.

Mama Duck said, "Quack, quack, quack, quack."
But only four little ducks came **waddling** back.

Four little ducks went out one day,
over the hills and far away.

Mama Duck said, "Quack, quack, quack, quack." But only three little ducks came waddling back.

Three little ducks went out one day,
over the hills and far away.

Mama Duck said, "Quack, quack, quack, quack."
But only two little ducks came waddling back.

Two little ducks went out one day,
over the hills and far away.

Mama Duck said, "Quack, quack, quack, quack."
But only one little duck came waddling back.

One little duck went out one day,
over the hills and far away.

Mama Duck said, "Quack, quack, quack, quack."
But no little ducks came waddling back.

Maybe if you "quack, quack, quack, quack" with Mama Duck, all of the little ducks will come back.

Ready?

No little ducks went out one day,
over the hills and far away.

Mama Duck said, "Quack, quack, quack, quack."
And all five little ducks came waddling back.

19

Five little ducks went out one day,
over the hills and far away.

Mama Duck said, "Quack, quack, quack, quack."
I wonder if any of our ducks will
come waddling back?

SONG LYRICS
Five Little Ducks

Five little ducks went out one day,
over the hills and far away.

Mama Duck said, "Quack, quack, quack, quack."
But only four little ducks came waddling back.

Four little ducks went out one day,
over the hills and far away.

Mama Duck said, "Quack, quack, quack, quack."
But only three little ducks came waddling back.

Three little ducks went out one day,
over the hills and far away.

Mama Duck said, "Quack, quack, quack, quack."
But only two little ducks came waddling back.

Two little ducks went out one day,
over the hills and far away.

Mama Duck said, "Quack, quack, quack, quack."
But only one little duck came waddling back.

One little duck went out one day,
over the hills and far away.

Mama Duck said, "Quack, quack, quack, quack."
But no little ducks came waddling back.

Maybe if you "quack, quack, quack, quack"
with Mama Duck, all of the little ducks will come
    back.

Ready?

"Quack! Quack! Quack! Quack!"

No little ducks went out one day,
over the hills and far away.

Mama Duck said, "Quack, quack, quack, quack."
And all five little ducks came waddling back.

Five little ducks went out one day,
over the hills and far away.

Mama Duck said, "Quack, quack, quack, quack."
I wonder if any of our ducks will come
    waddling back?

Five Little Ducks

Ska
Steven C Music

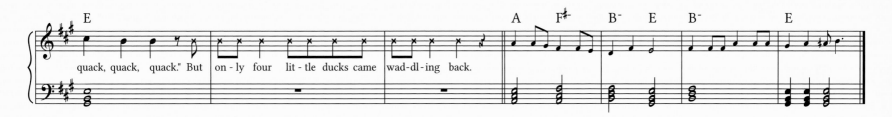

Lyrics:

Four little ducks went out one day,
over the hills and far away.
Mama Duck said, "Quack, quack, quack, quack."
But only three little ducks came waddling back.

Three little ducks went out one day,
over the hills and far away.
Mama Duck said, "Quack, quack, quack, quack."
But only two little ducks came waddling back.

Two little ducks went out one day,
over the hills and far away.
Mama Duck said, "Quack, quack, quack, quack."
But only one little duck came waddling back.

One little duck went out one day,
over the hills and far away.
Mama Duck said, "Quack, quack, quack, quack."
But no little ducks came waddling back.

Spoken:
Maybe if you "quack, quack, quack, quack"
with Mama Duck, all of the little ducks will come back.
Ready?
"Quack! Quack! Quack! Quack!"

No little ducks went out one day,
over the hills and far away.
Mama Duck said, "Quack, quack, quack, quack."
And all five little ducks came waddling back.

Five little ducks went out one day,
over the hills and far away.
Mama Duck said, "Quack, quack, quack, quack."
I wonder if any of our ducks will come waddling back?

GLOSSARY

ducklings—baby ducks

quack—the sound a duck makes

waddling—walking with short steps and a swaying motion

wander—to move from one place to another

GUIDED READING ACTIVITIES

1. The ducklings "wander" off. What does that mean? Where do they go?

2. Baby ducks are called ducklings. Can you think of names for other baby animals?

3. Squat down and fold your arms like wings. Now waddle around and quack like a duck. Is it hard to move this way?

TO LEARN MORE

Hammersmith, Craig. *Life in the Pond*. Mankato, MN: Capstone Press, 2012.

Moore, Eva. *Lucky Ducklings*. New York: Orchard Books, 2013.

Roth, Carol. *Five Little Ducklings Go to Bed*. New York: North-South Books Inc., 2013.

Rustad, Martha E. H. *A Baby Duck Story*. Mankato, MN: Capstone Press, 2012.